Bad Girls

Go Everywhere

Wisdom, Humor, and Inspiration
from Women with Attitude

Kathryn & Ross Petras

RUNNING PRESS
PHILADELPHIA · LONDON

Published by Running Press,
A Member of the Perseus Books Group

Printed in China

Books published by Running Press are available at special discounts for bulk purchases in the United States by corporations, institutions, and other organizations. For more informa-tion, please contact the Special Markets Department at the Perseus Books Group, 2300 Chestnut Street, Suite 200, Philadelphia, PA 19103, or call (800) 810-4145, ext. 5000, or e-mail special.markets@perseusbooks.com.

ISBN 978-0-7624-4866-1
Library of Congress Control Number: 2012944538

E-book ISBN 978-0-7624-4879-1

9   8   7   6   5   4   3   2   1
Digit on the right indicates the number of this printing

Cover and interior design by Jason Kayser
Edited by Jordana Tusman
Typography: Archer, Didot, and Neutra Text

Running Press Book Publishers
2300 Chestnut Street
Philadelphia, PA 19103-4371

Visit us on the web!
www.runningpress.com

Contents

Introduction

We're thrilled to introduce you to this collection of bad girls, bodacious babes, and tough chicks. Smart, funny, and inspirational women who can give you a virtual hug or a kick in the ass—depending on what you need.

It's a tough world, and women are out there dealing with it every day. Ok, so the economy may not be as strong as it could be; relationships are never as easy as they seem at the beginning; and problems at work are never far away. But most women are ready and able to take on life's challenges and emerge strong and triumphant at the other end. And more often than not, those triumphant women are the "bad girls"—the ones who don't obey every rule and who aren't anxious to please everyone. These are women who take and give abundantly, women who create their own way—whether others like it or not.

We can all be bad girls—embracing that inner toughness, proudly owning the word "bitch," and facing the world like the fierce females we are. It's just a matter of listening to that little voice inside. But all too often we're so immersed in relationships, work, daily routines, and social calendars that it's hard sometimes to hear our own thoughts or our own hearts. We are so often conditioned to do what's expected of us instead of breaking free and discovering what will help us meet our own personal fulfillment that we can lose our sense of vitality, creativity, and our essential true selves.

This is exactly why this collection of quotes exists, as a means and an inspiration for all of us to do better, reach higher, be happier, and face life with a determined mind and a sly grin—no matter what you're facing. Here, you'll find three hundred quotes from powerful women who can help get you going on your way! From Queen Victoria to Queen Latifah, from Bette Davis to Betty White, and from Maria Callas to Mindy Kaling, the women in this book share words of wisdom and humor on everything from men to work, from the meaning of life to romance, from sex to self-esteem, and so much more.

These quotes are meant to give you the empowerment, the inspiration, and the courage to take on whatever comes next. And, of course, to enjoy the process as you do. After all, good girls may be good—but bad girls are better!

Bad Girls,
Bitches, and Divas:

IT'S WHO WE ARE

It wasn't that long ago that women did not want to be called "bad girl," "bitch," or "diva." If you were called any of these names, it meant you were pushy, opinionated, and unladylike. Nowadays, many women proudly own these names—and it's something to celebrate!

To be good is to be forgotten. I'm going to be so bad I'll always be remembered.

Theda Bara (1885–1955)
American actress

I have bursts of being a lady, but it doesn't last long.

Shelley Winters (1920–2006)
American actress

If I were well behaved, I'd die of boredom.

Tallulah Bankhead (1902–1968)
American actress

Good girls go to heaven, bad girls go everywhere.

Mae West (1893–1980)
American actress and screenwriter

and Helen Gurley Brown (1922–2012)
American editor and writer

People are always like, "Oh, she's such a bitch."
I'm like, "Yeah, I am a bitch, actually."

Chelsea Handler (b. 1975)
American comedian, actress, and writer

I do have my standards. They're low, but I have them.

Bette Midler (b. 1945)
American singer and actress

Who are we? We are the life force
power of the universe...

Jill Bolte Taylor (b. 1959)
American scientist

Give a girl the right shoes, and she can conquer the world.

Marilyn Monroe (1926–1962)

American actress

I hope there's a tinge of disgrace about me.
Hopefully, there's one good scandal left in me yet.

Diana Rigg (b. 1938)
English actress

I'm a bad woman, but I'm damn good company.

Fanny Brice (1891–1951)
American comedian, singer, and actress

Send me flowers while I'm alive. They won't do me
a damn bit of good after I'm dead.

Joan Crawford (1905–1977)
American actress

It's fucking hard to be classy.

Janet Evanovich (b. 1943), in *One for the Money*
American writer

You can't fool an old bag like me.

Hedda Hopper (1885–1966)
American gossip columnist

I wish to live to 150 years old, but the
day I die, I wish it to be with a cigarette in one hand
and a glass of whiskey in the other.

Ava Gardner (1922–1990)
American actress

Yes, I swore, and I'm so fucking sorry.

Joan Rivers (b. 1933)
American comedian, actress, and TV personality

15

Jean Harlow *(trying on a dress)*:
Can you see through this?

Woman: I'm afraid you can, dear.

Harlow: I'll wear it.

Jean Harlow (1911–1937), in *Red-Headed Woman*
American actress

You teach 'em Mother Hubbard went to the
cupboard to get her poor dog a bone. I say, Mother
Hubbard had gin in that cupboard.

Moms Mabley (1894–1975)
American comedian

I won't be any properer than I have a mind to be.

Harriet Beecher Stowe (1811–1896)
American writer and abolitionist

I believe in trying everything once—except country dancing and incest.

Hermoine Gingold (1897–1987)
English actress

I don't pray. Kneeling bags my nylons.

Jan Sterling (1921–2004), in *Ace in the Hole*
American actress

No matter what happens, I'm loud, noisy, earthy, and ready for much more living.

I hate the word panties.
It's a cheesy word for underpants.

Katie Couric (b. 1957)
American journalist

Hell, I suppose if you stick around long enough
they have to say something nice about you.

Ava Gardner (1922–1990)
American actress

Whisky, gambling, and Ferraris are
better than housework.

Françoise Sagan (1935–2004)
French writer

I want to be a guy, but I want to wear a lot of makeup.

Gwen Stefani (b. 1969)
American singer, songwriter, and fashion designer

Ain't nobody going to censor me,
no sir! . . . at my age, honey, I can say what I want.

Annie Elizabeth Delaney (1891–1995)
American civil rights pioneer

What in heaven's name is strange
about a grandmother dancing nude? I'll bet
lots of grandmothers do it.

Sally Rand (1904–1979)
American actress and burlesque dancer

If you write anything nasty about me, I'll come around and blow up your toilet.

Courtney Love (b. 1964)
American singer, songwriter, and guitarist

I try not to drink too much because when I'm drunk, I bite.

Bette Midler (b. 1945)
American singer and actress

I know who you are, and I am not impressed.

Joan Jett (b. 1958)
American rock guitarist, singer, and songwriter

Tough girls come from New York. Sweet girls, they're from Georgia. But us Kentucky girls, we have fire and ice in our blood. We can ride horses, be a debutante, throw left hooks, and drink with the boys, all the while making sweet tea, darlin'. And if we have an opinion, you know you're gonna hear it.

Ashley Judd (b. 1968)
American actress

I'm famous for my modesty.
I'm famous for my gentility too. I'd like to see the cocksucker that says I'm not.

Lillian Hellman (1905–1985)
American writer

Q: What's the secret of
your longevity?

Julia Child:
Red meat and gin.

Julia Child (1912–2004)
American chef, writer, and TV personality

Go For It!:

INSPIRATION, FACING FEAR, AND THE KICK IN THE BUTT THAT YOU NEED

That first step is almost always the hardest, as the women quoted in this chapter know only too well. But they also know one of the greatest rules of life: when the time comes to take that first step, take it, damn it! And don't look back.

You can't be that kid standing at the top of the waterslide overthinking it. You have to go down the chute.

Tina Fey (b. 1970)
American actress, comedian, writer, and producer

The most effective way to do it, is to do it.

Amelia Earhart (1897–1939)
American aviation pioneer

Throw your dreams into space like a kite, and you do not know what it will bring back: a new life, a new friend, a new love, a new country.

Anaïs Nin (1903–1977)
French-Cuban writer

I have accepted fear as part of life—specifically the fear of change . . . I have gone ahead despite the pounding in the heart that says: turn back. . . .

Erica Jong (b. 1942)
American writer

Don't be afraid. Because you're
going to be afraid. But remember when you
become afraid, just don't be afraid.

Joan Jett (b. 1958)
American rock guitarist, singer, and songwriter

You don't need someone else's approval to do what
you want; just figure it out and do it, damn it!

Megan Mullally (b. 1958)
American actress

What's the worst that could happen?
Everyone turned me down; big deal.

J. K. Rowling (b. 1965)
English writer

I'm not intimidated
by anyone. Everyone
is made with two
arms, two legs, a stomach,
and a head. Just think
about that.

Josephine Baker (1906–1975)
American-French dancer and singer

Start thinking positively. You will notice a difference. Instead of "I think I'm a loser," try "I definitely am a loser." Stop being wishy-washy about things! How much more of a loser can you be if you don't even know you are one? Either you are a loser or you are not. Which is it, stupid?

Ellen DeGeneres (b. 1958)
American comedian, actress, writer, and talk show host

You must do the things you think you cannot do.

Eleanor Roosevelt (1884–1962)
American First Lady and humanitarian

You have to make more noise than anybody
else, you have to make yourself more obtrusive than
anybody else, you have to fill all the papers more
than anybody else, in fact, you have to be there all the
time and see that they do not snow you under.

Emmeline Pankhurst (1858–1928)
English political activist and suffragette

A champion is afraid of losing.
Everyone else is afraid of winning.

Billie Jean King (b. 1943)
American tennis player

Don't become something
just because someone
else wants you to, or because
it's easy; you won't be happy.
You have to do what you really,
really, really, really want
to do, even if it scares the
shit out of you.

Kristen Wiig (b. 1973)
American comedian, actress, and writer

Shape up, folks. There is no death.
Think of it as evolution.

Julie Newmar (b. 1933)
American actress

I'm here today because I refused to be unhappy.
I took a chance.

Wanda Sykes (b. 1964)
American comedian, actress, and writer

It is better to protest than to accept injustice.

Rosa Parks (1913–2005)
American civil rights activist

Walk the street with us into history.
Get off the sidewalk.

Dolores Huerta (b. 1930)
American labor leader and civil rights activist

If you don't risk anything, you risk even more.

Erica Jong (b. 1942)
American writer

Just put on your makeup and get out
there and do it.

Emma Bunton (b. 1976)
English singer

YOU GOT TO GET IT WHILE YOU CAN.

Janis Joplin (1943–1970)
American singer and songwriter

Life is a moveable feast . . . a tour in a post chaise, but who's to be considered as moving, it or you? The answer is: quick over the abyss, and be damned to being. Start doing.

Hortense Calisher (1911–2009)
American writer

A lot of people are waiting for Martin Luther King or Mahatma Gandhi to come back—but they are gone. We are it. It is up to us. It is up to you.

Marian Wright Edelman (b. 1939)
American children's rights activist

My favorite thing is to go where I've never been.

Diane Arbus (1923–1971)
American photographer

What the hell—you might be right,
you might be wrong, but don't just avoid.

Katharine Hepburn (1907–2003)
American actress

Now, get out there and kick ass!

Stella McCartney (b. 1971)
English fashion designer

Adventure is worthwhile in itself.

Amelia Earhart (1897–1939)
American aviation pioneer

Women and Men:

WHY ARE WOMEN SO STRANGE AND MEN SO WEIRD?

Science tells us that there are substantial psychological
differences between women and men. As scientist
Paul Irwing said, "They're almost like different species."
But haven't women always known that? Here, then, is a collection
of some of the most honest—and sometimes most snarky—
observations about strange women, weird men, and all
of our numerous and beguiling differences.

Girls, if a boy says something that isn't
funny, you don't have to laugh.

Amy Poehler (b. 1971)
American actress and comedian

You have to be very fond of men.
Very, very fond. You have to be very fond of
them to love them. Otherwise they're
simply unbearable.

Marguerite Duras (1914–1996)
French writer and film director

You know why God is a man?
Because if God was a woman she would have
made sperm taste like chocolate.

Carrie Snow (b. 1954)
American comedian

If women are supposed to be less rational and more emotional at the beginning of our menstrual cycle when the female hormone is at its lowest level, then why isn't it logical to say that, in those few days, women behave the most like the way men behave all month long?

Gloria Steinem (b. 1934)
American feminist and journalist

The trouble with some women is they get all excited over nothing—and then they marry him.

Cher (b. 1946)
American singer and actress

For me, cologne on men usually seals
my legs, not the deal.

Lizz Winstead (b. 1961)
American comedian and writer

Whatever women do they must do
twice as well as men to be thought half as good.
Luckily, this is not difficult.

Charlotte Whitton (1896–1975)
Canadian feminist and politician

Listen, if it's got four wheels or a dick,
you're going to have trouble with it, guaranteed.

Annie Proulx (b. 1935), in "A Lonely Coast"
American writer

I always say it was great for God to send his only son, but I'm waiting for him to send his only daughter. Then things will really be great.

Candace Pert (b. 1946)
American scientist

I love the male body—it's better designed than the male mind.

Andrea Newman (b. 1938)
English writer

I like the concept of "men." It's the reality I have problems with.

Stephanie Piro
American cartoonist

For most
of history,
Anonymous
was a
woman.

Virginia Woolf (1882–1941)
English writer

I like men to behave like men—strong and childish.

Françoise Sagan (1935-2004)
French writer

In my opinion, the only good spider is a dead spider,
and women's rights aren't worth dick if they mean I
can't ask a man to do my bug squashing.

Janet Evanovich (b. 1943), in *One for the Money*
American writer

When a man can't explain a woman's
actions, the first thing he thinks about is the
condition of her uterus.

Clare Booth Luce (1903-1987)
American writer and politician

A man is an accessory, like a pair of
earrings. It may finish the outfit, but you don't
really need it to keep you warm.

Rosemary Mittlemark
American writer

There are two types of women: those who
like chocolate and complete bitches.

Dawn French (b. 1957)
English actress and comedian

I believe that if a man does a job as well as a
woman, he should be paid as much.

Celeste Holm (1917–2012)
American actress

Most men would never tell a girl
her Pikachu smells like
a crab cake. It's just not done.
But they would have no qualms
about telling their guy friends.
Similarly, if you're a guy and you pull
your pants down, and the girl you're
with immediately starts text
messaging her friends, you have
a small penis.

Chelsea Handler (b. 1975)
American comedian, actress, and writer

All that you suspect about women's friendships is true. We talk about dick size.

Cynthia Heimel (b. 1947)
American writer

The men who constantly stare at our breasts are never the men we're attracted to.

Christina Hendricks (b. 1975)
American actress

I don't have a problem with men. I have a problem with STUPID men.

Maggie Estep (b. 1963)
American writer

I think men are very funny.
If I had one of those dangly things stuffed
down the front of my pants, I'd sit at
home all day laughing at myself.

Dawn French (b. 1957)
English actress, comedian, and writer

When a man gives his opinion,
he's a man. When a woman gives her opinion,
she's a bitch.

Bette Davis (1908–1989)
American actress

Rules to Live By:

ADVICE WITH ATTITUDE TO HELP YOU LIVE YOUR LIFE BADDER AND BETTER!

Yes, bad girls break the rules, but they also need some guidelines to help them make sense of this sometimes puzzling business of living. The point is that they do the picking. They choose what rules to obey and what rules to break. In this chapter, you'll find the rules some bad girls swear by.

If you obey all the rules you miss all the fun.

Katharine Hepburn (1907–2003)
American actress

Be nice to all assholes because it disables them!

Paula Pell
American writer, actress, and producer

If you can't change your fate, change your attitude.

Amy Tan (b. 1952)
American writer

Ignore the critics. Only mediocrity is safe from
ridicule. Dare to be different!

Dita Von Teese (b. 1972)
American burlesque dancer

This world is bullshit. And you shouldn't
model your life—wait a second—you
shouldn't model your life about what you think
that we think is cool and what we're wearing
and what we're saying and everything.
Go with yourself. Go with yourself.

Fiona Apple (b. 1977)
American singer and songwriter

If I had to live my life again, I'd make all the
same mistakes—only sooner.

Tallulah Bankhead (1902–1968)
American actress

Drama is very important in life: you have
to come on with a bang. You never want to
go out with a whimper. Everything can have drama
if it's done right. Even a pancake.

Julia Child (1912–2004)
American chef, writer, and TV personality

That whole generation that's gone now, that lived
through the two world wars, is a great example
to all of us. They knew how to live. If something bad
happened, they didn't sit at home, eat Häagen-Dazs, and
watch a movie. They got dressed up, went
out, caroused, and danced their feet off.

Sigourney Weaver (b. 1949)
American actress

Don't be mean, but don't settle either. Don't take shit.

Kristen Stewart (b. 1990)
American actress

Take all the rules away.
How can we live if we don't change?

Beyoncé (b. 1981)
American singer and songwriter

Why not seize the pleasure at once?
How often is happiness destroyed by preparation,
foolish preparation!

Jane Austen (1775–1817), in *Emma*
English writer

Life is like one big Mardi Gras. But instead of showing your boobs, show people your brain, and if they like what they see, you'll have more beads than you know what to do with.

Ellen DeGeneres (b. 1958)
American comedian, actress, writer, and talk show host

I've learned that you shouldn't go through
life with a catcher's mitt on both hands; you need to
be able to throw something back.

Maya Angelou (b. 1928)
American writer

Don't compromise yourself. You're all you've got.

Janis Joplin (1943–1970)
American singer and songwriter

Let your soul do the singin'.

Ma Rainey (1886–1939)
American singer

God will protect us, but to make sure, carry
a heavy club.

Gypsy Rose Lee (1911–1970)
American burlesque dancer

Never wound a snake; kill it.

Harriet Tubman (1820–1913)
American abolitionist

Life is like a game of poker: if you don't put any in
the pot, there won't be any to take out.

Moms Mabley (1894–1975)
American comedian

Lesson learned? When people say, "You really, really must" do something, it means you don't really have to. No one ever says, "You really, really must deliver the baby during labor." When it's true, it doesn't need to be said.

Tina Fey (b. 1970)
American actress, comedian, writer, and producer

If you don't want to do something, you should say, "I don't want to do it."

Heather Locklear (b. 1961)
American actress

I'm not insecure. I've been through way
too much fucking shit to be insecure. I've got huge balls.
But I've been humbled. That makes you
grateful for every day you have.

Drew Barrymore (b. 1975)
American actress

You need to do everything possible to
stand out or commit to fitting in. I'd say, just own
your sluttiness. Just own it.

Emma Stone (b. 1988)
American actress

HOSS, IF YOU CAN'T DO IT WITH FEELING— DON'T.

Patsy Cline (1932–1963)
American singer

Be bold. If you're going to make an error, make a doozy, and don't be afraid to hit the ball.

Billie Jean King (b. 1943)
American tennis player

There is always something to do. There are hungry people to feed, naked people to clothe, sick people to comfort and make well. And while I don't expect you to save the world, I do think it's not asking too much for you to love those with whom you sleep, share the happiness of those whom you call friend, engage those among you who are visionary, and remove from your life those who offer you depression, despair, and disrespect.

Nikki Giovanni (b. 1943)
American writer

If you're going to do something
wrong, do it big, because the punishment is the
same either way.

Jayne Mansfield (1933–1967)
American actress

Life loves to be taken by the lapel
and told: "I am with you, kid. Let's go."

Maya Angelou (b. 1928)
American writer

Make this weekend count: kiss some cute faces, ignore
some assholes, and wave at a lot of old people.

Paula Pell
American writer, actress, and producer

Pray for the dead and fight like hell for the living.

Mary Harris "Mother" Jones (1837–1930)
American political activist

Always remember this: there are
only eighteen inches between a pat on the back
and a kick in the rump.

Hattie McDaniel (1895–1952)
American actress

Laugh at yourself first, before anyone else can.

Elsa Maxwell (1883–1963)
American gossip columnist

Wouldn't it be terrible if you'd spent all your life doing everything you were supposed to do— didn't drink, didn't smoke, didn't eat things, took lots of exercise—all the things you didn't want to do, and suddenly one day you were run over by a big red bus, and as the wheels were crunching into you you'd say, "Oh my god, I could have got so drunk last night!" That's the way you should live your life, as if tomorrow you'll be run over by a big red bus.

Queen Mother Elizabeth (1900–2002)
English monarch

Women at Work:

SHE WORKS HARD FOR THE MONEY

Whether we work for a huge corporation or in a small store, whether we're self-employed or a stay-at-home mom, we're all working our asses off. And there's definitely a right way to do it, at least according to these tough chicks who know what they're worth and aren't afraid to let the boss—and everyone else—know.

Sometimes you have to be a bitch to get things done.

Madonna (b. 1958)
American singer and songwriter

Do stuff you will enjoy thinking about
and telling stories about for many years to come.
Do stuff you will want to brag about.

Rachel Maddow (b. 1973)
American TV host and political commentator

I didn't want to be nobody's damn maid.

Billie Holiday (1915–1959)
American singer and songwriter

What I wanted to be when I grew up was—in charge.

Wilma Vaught (b. 1930)
United States Air Force Brigadier General

You can fool all of the people some of the time and some of the people all of the time. And that's sufficient.

Rose King (1884–1967)
American actress

I don't know much about being a millionaire, but I'll bet I'd be darling at it.

Dorothy Parker (1893–1967)
American writer

You have the gift of time. Use it to do what you love. Believe anything is possible, and then work like hell to make it happen.

Julianna Margulies (b. 1966)
American actress

Success didn't spoil me; I've always
been insufferable.

Fran Lebowitz (b. 1950)
American writer

I'm a maniacal perfectionist. And if I weren't,
I wouldn't have this company.

Martha Stewart (b. 1941)
American lifestyle expert and talk show host

For a woman, the quickest path to
success is to do something all other women hate
so much they blog about it.

Sarah Thyre (b. 1968)
American actress and writer

She said I was afraid of success, which may in fact be true, because I have a feeling that fulfilling my potential would really cut into my sittin' around time.

Maria Bamford (b. 1970)
American comedian

I do want to get rich but I never want to do what there is to do to get rich.

Gertrude Stein (1874–1946)
American writer

Money may not buy happiness, but I'd rather cry in a Jaguar than on a bus.

Françoise Sagan (1935–2004)
French writer

I think the only reason
that I'm still goin' now is that I don't
listen. I think you can't listen.
You listen to what works and
what doesn't work for you and you
just ignore people. Understand where
it is you want to go. Then picture
yourself there. If you can picture
yourself there, then you
can be there. Bottom line.

Cyndi Lauper (b. 1953)
American singer and songwriter

Always be the only person who can sign your checks.

Oprah Winfrey (b. 1954)
American talk show host, producer, actress, and philanthropist

For the better part of my childhood,
my professional aspirations were simple—I wanted
to be an intergalactic princess.

Janet Evanovich (b. 1943), in *Seven Up*
American writer

When you don't make moves, and when
you don't climb up the ladder, everybody loves you
because you're not competition.

Nicki Minaj (b. 1982)
American singer

When other little girls wanted to be ballet dancers,
I kind of wanted to be a vampire.

Angelina Jolie (b. 1975)
American actress and humanitarian

Grit your teeth, because it is a matter
of resilience, stamina, and energy. And never
try to imitate what the boys do.

Christine Lagarde (b. 1956)
Managing Director of the International Monetary Fund

There is no point at which you can say,
"Well, I'm successful now. I might as well take a nap."

Carrie Fisher (b. 1956)
American actress and writer

I don't like to gamble, but if there's one thing I'm willing to bet on, it's myself.

Beyoncé (b. 1981)
American singer and songwriter

I have never worked a day in
my life without selling. If I believe in something,
I sell it, and I sell it hard.

Estée Lauder (1906–2004)
American businesswoman

Nearly every glamorous, wealthy,
successful career woman you might envy now
started out as some kind of schlep.

Helen Gurley Brown (1922–2012)
American magazine publisher and writer

Never worry about the facts.
Just present an image to the public.

Diana Vreeland (1903–1989)
American fashion editor

No one asked you to be happy. Get to work.

Colette (1873–1954)
French writer

I had to slug my way up in a town called
Hollywood where people love to trample you to death.
I don't relax because I don't know how. I don't want to
know how. Life is too short to relax.

Susan Hayward (1917–1975)
American actress

I used to want the words "She tried" on my tombstone. Now I want "She did it."

Katherine Dunham (1909–2006)
American dancer and choreographer

When given the choice between fame and glory, take glory. Glory has a way of sneaking up on fame and stealing its lunch money later anyway.

Rachel Maddow (b. 1973)
American TV host and political commentator

I believe you are your work. Don't trade
the stuff of your life, time, for nothing more than dollars.
That's a rotten bargain.

Rita Mae Brown (b. 1944)
American writer

Some people think they are worth a lot of
money just because they have it.

Fannie Hurst (1889–1968)
American writer

Lovers, Friends, Enemies, and Frenemies:

UNDERSTANDING THE ONES YOU LOVE
AND THE ONES YOU LOVE TO HATE

What's the secret to dealing with all those people in this big, wicked world—from dear lovers to deadly enemies? Bad girls know the answer. They begin with an uncompromising look at humanity and end with the courage to accept individuals exactly as they are, no pretenses. Therein lie freedom and happy relationships—or at least honest ones.

Love is or it ain't. Thin love ain't love at all.

Toni Morrison (b. 1931)
American writer

I'm selfish, impatient, and a little insecure. I make mistakes, I am out of control, and at times hard to handle. But if you can't handle me at my worst, then you sure as hell don't deserve me at my best.

Marilyn Monroe (1926–1962)
American actress

Lovers have a right to betray you . . . friends don't.

Judy Holliday (1921–1965)
American actress

They say you shouldn't say anything about the dead unless it's good. He's dead. Good.

Moms Mabley (1894–1975)
American comedian

It's the friends you can call up at 4:00 a.m. that matter.

Marlene Dietrich (1901–1992)
German-American actress and singer

The older you get, the fewer slumber parties
there are, and I hate that. I liked slumber parties.
What happened to them?

Drew Barrymore (b. 1975)
American actress

Lots of people want to ride with you in
the limo, but what you want is someone who will take
the bus with you when the limo breaks down.

Oprah Winfrey (b. 1954)
American talk show host, producer, actress, and philanthropist

I leave before being left. I decide.

Brigitte Bardot (b. 1934)
French fashion model, actress, and singer

The problem with people who have no vices is that generally you can be pretty sure they're going to have some pretty annoying virtues.

Elizabeth Taylor (1932–2011)
American actress

When you're your own person and not so concerned with impressing, then the other person is very impressed.

Madonna (b. 1958)
American singer and songwriter

I think, therefore I am single.

Lizz Winstead (b. 1961)
American comedian and writer

Love is an illusion; it is the world's greatest mistake. I ought to know for I've been loved as no other woman of my time has been loved. Men have threatened suicide, they have taken poison, they have fought duels for me. All kinds have come to me—geniuses, poets, millionaires, artists, musicians—but now there is not one to whom I have appealed for the loan of £25 who have responded. There is love for you!

Isadora Duncan (1877–1927)
American dancer

Markoe's Axiom: the person who tells you that they broke up a relationship because the other person was crazy is almost always crazy too.

Merrill Markoe (b. 1948)
American writer and comedian

I've always said to my men friends, "If you really care for me, darling, you will give me territory." Give me land, give me land.

Eartha Kitt (1927–2008)
American singer and actress

I like the jewelry part of getting married, but I can buy my own damn rings, too.

Queen Latifah (b. 1970)
American singer and actress

I've learned one hell of a lot about
men in my lifetime. They're all right to take to
bed, but you sure better never let them get a
stranglehold on you.

Blaze Starr (b. 1932)
American stripper and burlesque dancer

Men always think I'm too demanding . . . but all I ask is
that they treat me like the goddess I am.

Kathy Shaskan
American writer and cartoonist

I want a man who's kind and understanding.
Is that too much to ask of a millionaire?

Zsa Zsa Gabor (b. 1917)
Hungarian-American actress

I urge you all today, especially today during
these times of chaos and war, to love yourself
without reservations and to love each other without
restraint. Unless you're into leather.

Margaret Cho (b. 1968)
American comedian, writer, and actress

I don't like girls whining and complaining about wanting a man! . . . It is just not up my alley. I don't believe in it. There is nothing you can control about love. Somebody once said, "Everything you want in the world is just right outside your comfort zone." *Everythingyoucouldpossiblywant!*

Jennifer Aniston (b. 1969)
American actress

I've married a few people I shouldn't have, but haven't we all?

Mamie Van Doren (b. 1931)
American actress

Self-Image and Sass:

THE WOMAN IN YOUR MIRROR,
THE WOMAN IN YOUR MIND

Look at yourself in the mirror—what do you see?
The women quoted in this chapter have looked in the
mirror and gone beyond petty body issues and
self-image problems and paralyzing doubts. They accept
who they see looking back at them, and more
importantly, they *like* who they see.

The important thing is not what they think of
me but what I think of them.

Queen Victoria (1819–1901)
English monarch

Teenage girls, please don't worry about being super popular in high school, or being the best actress in high school, or the best athlete. Not only do people not care about any of that the second you graduate, but when you get older, if you reference your successes in high school too much, it actually makes you look kind of pitiful, like some babbling old Tennessee Williams character with nothing else going on in her current life. What I've noticed is that almost no one who was a big star in high school is a big star later in life. For us overlooked kids, it's so wonderfully fair.

Mindy Kaling (b. 1979)
American actress, comedian, and writer

I do the best I can. Everything else is everybody else's problem.

Alison Janney (b. 1959)
American actress

Enjoy the power and beauty of your youth. Trust me: in twenty years, you'll look back at photos of yourself and recall in a way you can't grasp now how much possibility lay before you and how fabulous you really looked. You are not as fat as you imagine.

Mary Schmich (b. 1953)
American journalist

I advocate

glamour.

Every day.
Every minute.

Dita Von Teese (b. 1972)
American burlesque dancer

If people make fun of you, you must be doing something right.

Amy Lee (b. 1981)
American singer and songwriter

No one can make you feel inferior without your consent.

Eleanor Roosevelt (1884–1962)
American First Lady and humanitarian

Sometimes I have the most amazing moments of clarity. Razor sharp, crystal clear. It's at these times I can see how fucking stupid I am.

Tracey Emin (b. 1963)
English artist

So, it's just no hope. I can't be cool.
I tried with the giant sunglasses—no dice. Sorry.
I remain dorky forever. So—it's okay.

Ysabella Brave (b. 1979)
American singer

I'm a get-a-dress-at-the-thrift-shop-
but-open-a-bottle-of-champagne kind of person.

Helen Mirren (b. 1945)
English actress

Any girl can be glamorous. All you have to do
is stand still and look stupid.

Hedy Lamarr (1913–2000)
Austrian-American actress and inventor

I think the reward for conformity is that everyone likes you except yourself.

Rita Mae Brown (b. 1944)
American writer

It's okay to be fat. So you're fat. Just be fat and shut up about it.

Roseanne Barr (b. 1952)
American actress, comedian, writer, and producer

If you retain nothing else, always remember the most important rule of beauty, which is: who cares?

Tina Fey (b. 1970)
American actress, comedian, writer, and producer

I don't like myself, I'm crazy about myself.

Mae West (1893–1980)
American actress and screenwriter

It's not until you fight for something that you become who you are.

Sigourney Weaver (b. 1949)
American actress

Do you really have to be the ice queen intellectual or the slut whore? Isn't there some way to be both?

Susan Sarandon (b. 1946)
American actress

A forty-one-inch
bust and a lot
of perseverance will
get you more than a
cup of coffee—a
lot more.

Jayne Mansfield (1933–1967)
American actress

I ain't good lookin', but I'm somebody's angel child.

Bessie Smith (1894–1937), in "Reckless Blues"
American singer (lyric by Fred Longshaw and Jack Gee)

I'm just a good strong Louisiana woman
who can cook rice so every grain stands by itself.

Mahalia Jackson (1911–1972)
American singer

Hold your head high and sway your hips
when you walk!

Christina Aguilera (b. 1980)
American singer

Get rid of those terrible jeans that everybody
else wears. And wear something different for a change,
so you don't just look like a clone.

Vivienne Westwood (b. 1941)
English fashion designer

I do think that if you like lipstick or watch *Keeping Up
with the Kardashians* while you do the elliptical
machine, and you're willing to admit to any of that,
that there are people who think you're letting down
women or something. Which is just a bunch of bullshit
and can make me kind of angry. I don't get it.

Mindy Kaling (b. 1979)
American actress, comedian, and writer

Don't be humble. You're not that great.

Golda Meir (1898–1978)
First female Prime Minister of Israel

Does Mary Poppins have an orgasm?
Does she go to the bathroom? I assure you, she does.

Julie Andrews (b. 1935)
English actress and singer

I have always been famous—you just didn't know it yet.

Lady Gaga (b. 1986)
American singer and songwriter

I'm not playing a role. I'm being myself,
whatever the hell that is.

Bea Arthur (1922–2009)
American actress

I've always wondered what it would be
like if somebody from outer space landed with
three heads. Then all of a sudden everybody else
wouldn't look so bad, huh? Well, okay,
you're a little different from me but, hey, ya
got one head.

Cyndi Lauper (b. 1953)
American singer and songwriter

My legs aren't so beautiful.

I just know what to do with them.

Marlene Dietrich (1901–1992)
German-American actress and singer

My father was a proctologist, and my mother
an abstract artist, that's how I
view the world.

Sandra Bernhard (b. 1955)
American comedian, singer, and actress

Every day, I define myself. I know who I am today.
I don't promise you anything for tomorrow.

Salma Hayek (b. 1966)
Mexican-American actress

Trust yourself. Think for yourself.
Act for yourself. Speak for yourself. Be yourself.
Imitation is suicide.

Marva Collins (b. 1936)
American educator

You are more powerful than you know;
you are beautiful just as you are.

Melissa Etheridge (b. 1961)
American singer and songwriter

I'M THE NICEST GODDAMN DAME THAT EVER LIVED.

Bette Davis (1908–1989)
American actress

Womanly Wisdom:

WITTY, FIERCE, AND UNCOMPROMISING TRUTHS ABOUT THE WORLD

In folklore, an older woman, a crone, often shares her wisdom with the young, helping them make their way through the world. Well, the women below are definitely not crones, but they are certainly wise. Here, they share the insights they've discovered through living life head-on— with passion, with humor, and with strength.

The big secret in life is that there is no big secret.

Oprah Winfrey (b. 1954)
American talk show host, producer, actress, and philanthropist

If you're looking for wisdom, call your grandmother.

Alice Hoffman (b. 1952)
American writer

Stupid people are dangerous.

Suzanne Collins (b. 1962), in *The Hunger Games*
American writer

I begin to think that a calm is not desirable in any situation in life. Every object is beautiful in motion; a ship under sail, trees gently agitated with the wind, and a fine woman dancing are three instances in point. Man was made for action and for bustle, too, I believe.

Abigail Adams (1744–1818)
American First Lady

Nothing is ever enough when what
you are looking for isn't what you really want.

Arianna Huffington (b. 1950)
American journalist

Treating the whole world as if it works for
you doesn't suggest you're special, it
means you're an ass.

Raina Kelley
American journalist

Ever notice how "What the hell" is always
the right answer?

Marilyn Monroe (1926–1962)
American actress

I wanted to believe,
and I tried my damnedest
to believe in the rainbow
I tried to get over, and
I couldn't! So what? Lots
of people can't!

Judy Garland (1922–1969)
American singer and actress

Life will break you. Nobody can protect you from that, and living alone won't either, for solitude will also break you with its yearning. You have to love. You have to feel. It is the reason you are here on earth. You are here to risk your heart. You are here to be swallowed up. And when it happens that you are broken, or betrayed, or left, or hurt, or death brushes near, let yourself sit by an apple tree and listen to the apples falling all around you in heaps, wasting their sweetness. Tell yourself you tasted as many as you could.

Louise Erdrich (b. 1954), in *The Painted Drum*
American writer

All the dreamers in all the world are dizzy in the noodle.

Edie Adams (1927–2008)
American singer, actress, and comedian

We're all idiots when we're young.
We don't think we are, but we are. So we should be.

Helen Mirren (b. 1945)
English actress

I'll match my flops with anybody's but I
wouldn't have missed 'em.

Rosalind Russell (1907–1976)
American actress

I have very often deprived myself
of the necessities of life, but I have never
consented to give up a luxury.

Colette (1873–1954)
French writer

You can be up to
your boobies in white
satin, with gardenias in your
hair and no sugar cane
for miles, but you
can still be working on a
plantation.

Billie Holiday (1915–1959)
American singer and songwriter

Take your life in your own hands and what happens?
A terrible thing: no one to blame.

Erica Jong (b. 1942)
American writer

Dreck is dreck and no amount of
fancy polish is going to make it anything else.

Linda Ellerbee (b. 1944)
American journalist

The most common way people give up their power
is by thinking they don't have any.

Alice Walker (b. 1944)
American writer

A lot of people are afraid to say what they want. That's why they don't get what they want.

Madonna (b. 1958)
American singer and songwriter

Tomorrow never happens, man. It's all the same fucking day, man.

Janis Joplin (1943–1970) in "Ball and Chain"
American singer and songwriter (lyric by Mike Ness)

No matter how big or soft or warm your bed is, you still have to get out of it.

Grace Slick (b. 1939)
American singer and songwriter

Sometimes you have to sacrifice your performance for high heels.

Gwen Stefani (b. 1969)
American singer, songwriter, and fashion designer

I wanted a perfect ending. Now I've learned, the hard way, that some poems don't rhyme, and some stories don't have a clear beginning, middle, and end. Life is about not knowing, having to change, taking the moment and making the best of it, without knowing what's going to happen next. Delicious ambiguity.

Gilda Radner (1946–1989)
American comedian

If you're forty years old and you've never had a failure, you've been deprived.

Gloria Swanson (1899–1983)
American actress

Always remember: if you're alone in the kitchen and you drop the lamb, you can always just pick it up. Who's going to know?

Julia Child (1912–2004)
American chef, writer, and TV personality

The reality is that we're all in the wilderness and we have to survive on our own, and things constantly change, and if we don't accept that, then we're just trying to fool ourselves. But the beauty of wilderness is that sometimes you can wake up in the morning and feel so sweet and whole.

Sophie B. Hawkins (b. 1967)
American singer and songwriter

The truth will set you free. But first, it will piss you off.

Gloria Steinem (b. 1934)
American feminist and journalist

Life sucks. Get over it.

Sarah Dessen (b. 1970), in *Keeping the Moon*
American writer

The whole thing of clothes is insane. You can spend a dollar on a jacket in a thrift store. And you can spend a thousand dollars on a jacket in a shop. And if you saw those two jackets walking down the street, you probably wouldn't know which was which.

Helen Mirren (b. 1945)
English actress

Security is mostly a superstition.
It does not exist in nature . . . Life is either a daring
adventure or nothing at all.

Helen Keller (1880–1968)
American writer, political activist, and humanitarian

The truth does not change according to
our ability to stomach it.

Flannery O'Connor (1925–1964)
American writer

You may not be able to change the world, but at
least you can embarrass the guilty.

Jessica Mitford (1917–1996)
English writer

People
have the
power
to redeem
the work
of fools.

Patti Smith (b. 1946), in "People Have the Power"
American singer and songwriter

Sex:

INSIGHTS FROM UNDER THE COVERS

A recent book by two psychologists stated that
women have sex for exactly 237 different reasons. "Funny,"
the bad girls quoted below would probably say,
"We have sex for only one reason: we want to. But we've
got more than 237 things to say about it." And
here are a few of the best.

When I'm good, I'm very, very good, but
when I'm bad, I'm better.

Mae West (1893–1980)
American actress and screenwriter

Women can fake orgasms, but men can
fake whole relationships.

Sharon Stone (b. 1958)
American actress, film producer, and former model

Ducking for apples—change one letter and it's
the story of my life.

Dorothy Parker (1893–1967)
American writer

I've tried several varieties of sex. The conventional position makes me claustrophobic and the others give me a stiff neck or lockjaw.

Tallulah Bankhead (1902–1968)
American actress

Men don't realize that if we're sleeping with them on the first date, we're probably not interested in seeing them again either.

Chelsea Handler (b. 1975)
American comedian, actress, and writer

I think it is funny
that we were freer
about sexuality in the
fourth century B.C.
It is a little
disconcerting.

Angelina Jolie (b. 1975)
American actress and humanitarian

A man on a date wonders if he'll get lucky.
The woman already knows.

Monica Piper
American comedian and writer

I have never liked bargains when it came to sex.

Hedy Lamarr (1913–2000)
Austrian-American actress and inventor

An orgasm is a way of saying you
enjoyed yourself, even as you compliment a host
on a wonderful spinach quiche.

Helen Gurley Brown (1922–2012)
American magazine publisher and writer

It takes a good girl to be bad.

Sophie Tucker (1886–1966)
American singer

A woman with a well stocked toy
drawer isn't dependent on anyone and is unlikely to
hurl herself at a lowlife just for nooky.

Arianne Cohen (b. 1981)
American writer

I love sex as much as I love music, and I think
it's as hard to do.

Linda Ronstadt (b. 1946)
American singer

Forget about the mind.
The clitoris is a terrible thing to waste.

Lisa Kogan (b. 1962)
American writer

It's ill-becoming for an old broad to sing about how
bad she wants it. But occasionally we do.

Lena Horne (1917–2010)
American singer, actress, and civil rights activist

Sex is hardly ever just about sex.

Shirley MacLaine (b. 1934)
American actress and writer

You can think clearly only with your clothes on.

Margaret Atwood (b. 1939), in *The Handmaid's Tale*
Canadian writer

When feeling cheap and nasty,
remind yourself that without infidelity, literature
and opera would be up shit creek.

Kathy Lette (b. 1958)
Australian writer

Sex is a bad thing because it rumples the clothes.

Jacqueline Kennedy Onassis (1929–1994)
American First Lady and editor

NO ONE EVER EXPECTS A GREAT LAY TO PAY ALL THE BILLS.

Jean Harlow (1911-1937)
American actress

My problem is, I'm a hell of a nice dame.
The most horrible whores are famous. I did what I did
for love. The others did it for money.

Hedy Lamarr (1914–2000)
Austrian-American actress and inventor

Sex is like a bridge game; if you don't have
a good partner, you better have a good hand.

Mae West (1893–1980)
American actress and screenwriter

I don't think I'm gay. I don't think I'm straight.
I think I'm just slutty. Where's my parade?

Margaret Cho (b. 1968)
American comedian, writer, and actress

For women, the best aphrodisiacs are
words. The G-spot is in the ears. He who looks for
it below there is wasting his time.

Isabel Allende (b. 1942), in *Of Love and Shadows*
Chilean writer

Kicking Ass:

TOUGH CHICKS TELL IT LIKE IT IS

Sometimes a woman has to kick some ass—someone else's ass or her own. Here, in their own words, is a dose of tough, straight talk from bad girls at their worst—or is it at their best? Telling off enemies, enjoying the fight, saying it like it is—all with a healthy dose of attitude.

Girls got balls. They're just a little higher up, that's all.

Joan Jett (b. 1958)
American rock guitarist, singer, and songwriter

Keep fighting for freedom and justice, beloveds, but don't you forget to have fun doin' it. Lord, let your laughter ring forth. Be outrageous, ridicule the 'fraidy-cats, rejoice in all the oddities that freedom can produce. And when you get through kickin' ass and celebratin' the sheer joy of a good fight, be sure to tell those who come after how much fun it was.

Molly Ivins (1944–2007)
American journalist

All right, muffin. Let's have a dose of straight talk.

Thelma Ritter (1902–1969), in *Pickup on South Street*
American actress

One of my missions on earth is to tell people
how full of shit they are.

Roseanne Barr (b. 1952)
American actress, comedian, writer, and producer

A tough girl, more than anything else, is a
girl who doesn't care if you're shocked . . . A tough girl
doesn't sit like a lady or laugh like a little girl.
She goes where she shouldn't, and when
she gets there, she does exactly what she wants—
and she likes it.

Claudia Shear (b. 1962), in *Dirty Blonde*
American actress and writer

Don't fuck with me, fellas— This ain't my first time at the rodeo!

Joan Crawford (1905–1977), in *Mommy Dearest*
American actress

The easiest thing in the world is to be
smart-alecky and cynical and snide and jaded.
It's hard to keep your heart open.

Fannie Flagg (b. 1944)
American actress and writer

I can whistle through my fingers, bulldog
a steer, light a fire with two sticks, shoot a pistol with
fair accuracy, set type, and teach school. . . .

Ann Sheridan (1915–1967)
American actress

Drive on! We'll sweep up the blood later!

Katharine Hepburn (1907–2003)
American actress

There was one of two things I had a right to: liberty or death. If I could not have one, I would have the other; for no man should take me alive.

Harriet Tubman (1820–1913)
American abolitionist

Women who pay their own rent don't have to be nice.

Katherine Dunn (b. 1945)
American writer

Strength is the capacity to break a Hershey bar into four pieces with your bare hands— and then eat just one of the pieces.

Judith Viorst (b. 1931)
American writer

THEY CAN'T SCARE ME, IF I SCARE THEM FIRST.

Lady Gaga (b. 1986)
American singer and songwriter

Whenever anyone has called me a bitch, I have taken it as a compliment. To me, a bitch is assertive, unapologetic, demanding, intimidating, intelligent, fiercely protective, in control—all very positive attributes. But it's not supposed to be a compliment, because there's that old, stupid double standard: When men are aggressive and dominant, they are admired, but when a woman possesses those same qualities, she is dismissed and called a bitch.

Margaret Cho (b. 1968)
American comedian, writer, and actress

People wish their enemies dead, but I do not; I say, give them the gout, give them the stone!

Mary Wortley Montagu (1689–1762)
English aristocrat and writer

I couldn't give a rat's tutu about your emotional distress.

Judge Judy Sheindlin (b. 1942)
American judge and TV personality

It's like I tell people at my stand-up shows: by making me a bitch, you have given me my freedom, the freedom to say and do things I couldn't do if I was "a nice girl" with some sort of stupid, goody-two-shoes image to keep up. Things that require courage. Things that require balls. Things that need to be done. By making me a bitch, you have freed me from the trite, sexist, bourgeois prison of "likeability." Any idiot can be liked. It takes talent to scare the crap out of people.

Alison Arngrim (b. 1962)
American actress and writer

I FOUND MY INNER BITCH AND RAN WITH HER.

Courtney Love (b. 1964)
American singer, songwriter, and musician

Most chick singers say, "If you hurt me, I'll die."
I say, "If you hurt me, I'll kick your ass."

Pat Benatar (b. 1953)
American singer

If anyone ever catches me believing in
anything, I hope they give me a good sock in the jaw.

Joan Crawford (1905–1977)
American actress

I'd never been a good damsel in distress.
I was a "hands-on" damsel.

Jennifer Armintrout (b. 1980), in *Possession*
American writer

Are we bitches because we have our own opinions? If that makes me a bitch, or that makes women bitches, then maybe we're all bitches.

Zooey Deschanel (b. 1980)
American actress and singer

Go and tell that nasty, rude little princess that we've known each other for long enough and gabbed enough in ladies' rooms that she should skip the ho-hum royal routine and just pop over here and ask me herself. Tell her I'll sing if she christens a ship first.

Judy Garland (1922–1969)
American singer and actress

Life's a bitch. You've got to go out and kick ass.

Maya Angelou (b. 1928)
American writer

As a woman, I find it very embarrassing
to be in a meeting and realize I'm the only one
in the room with balls.

Rita Mae Brown (b. 1944)
American writer

Don't talk to me about rules, dear. Wherever I stay,
I make the goddamn rules.

Maria Callas (1923–1977)
Greek singer

I shall be an autocrat: that's my trade.
And the good Lord will forgive me: that's his.

Catherine the Great (1729–1796)
Russian monarch

I know I have the body but of a weak and
feeble woman; but I have the heart and stomach of
a king, and of a king of England, too.

Queen Elizabeth I (1533–1603)
English monarch

People say to me, "You're not very feminine."
Well, they can suck my dick.

Roseanne Barr (b. 1952)
American actress, comedian, writer, and producer

I've never had a humble opinion.
If you've got an opinion, why be humble about it?

Joan Baez (b. 1941)
American singer and songwriter

YOU DON'T LUCK INTO INTEGRITY. YOU WORK AT IT.

Betty White (b. 1922), in *If You Ask Me*
American actress

Photo Credits